God's Little Instruction Book
for the Workplace

P.O. Box 55388
Tulsa, OK 74155

God's Little Instruction Book for the Workplace
IBSN 1-56292-103-7
Copyright © 1995 by Honor Books, Inc.
P.O. Box 55388
Tulsa, Oklahoma 74155

Acknowledgments

We acknowledge and thank the following people for the quotes used in this book: John D. Rockefeller, Jr. (7), Dr. Eugene Swearingen(8), Winston Churchill (9, 65), Katherine Graham (10), Arnold Bennett (11), Peter J. Daniels (12), Samuel Johnson (13, 76, 99), Benjamin Franklin (14, 82), Lillian Dickson (15), Cervantes (16, 25), Michelangelo (17), Don Herold (18), Zig Ziglar (19, 51), Jean Sibelius (20), Harvey MacKay (21), Sebasstien-Roche (22), Ralph Waldo Emerson (24, 81), Johann Wolfgang von Goethe (26, 109, 128), Henry David Thoreau (27), Dennis Waitley (28, 131), Friedrich Wilhelm Nietzsche (29, 38), James Huxley (30), Diane Ravitch (31), Roger von Oech (32), Dwight D. Eisenhower (33, 88), Mark Twain (34, 41), St. Francis de Sales (35, 77), E.M. Kelly (36), Henry Ford (39, 107), Aeschylus (40), Gorden van Sauter (43), Margaret Fuller (44), William James (45), Edward Gibson (46), Solon Bale (47), Elbert Hubbard (49, 108), Bessie Stanley (50), David J. Schwartz (53), St. Francis Xavier (54), John A. Shedd (55), Lucius Annaeus Seneca (56), George Herbert Palmer (57), William Feather (58), Isaac Singer (59), a Jesuit motto (60), Lawrence D. Bell (61), George Herbert (63), Bill Cosby (64), J.R.R. Tolkien (66), Robert Frost (68), Marcel Pagnol (69), Charles Dickens (71), Euripides (73), Martin Luther King, Jr. (74), Milton S.

Gould (75), William Carey (78), Robert Browning (79), Catherine Booth (80), Jim Rohn (83), Edward Young (84), Sam Snead (85), David Mahoney (86), Mary Webb (87), G.K. Chesterton (89, 153), William Jennings Bryan (90), Horace Walpole (91), Theodore Roosevelt (92, 98), Baltasar Gracian (93), Ronald E. Osborn (95), Diane Sawyer (96), Helen Keller (97), Lao-Tze (100), Michael Aspen (101), Abraham Lincoln (103), H.L. Menken (105), Bertolt Brecht (106), Marcus Aurelius (110), George S. Patton (111), Thomas Alva Edison (112, 132), John Wayne (113), Gerald R. Ford (114), Thomas Fuller (115), Horace (116), Woodrow Wilson (117), William Danforth (118), George P. Burnham (119), James L. Hayes (120), Robert Mitchum (121), Ronald Brown (123), Barbara Baruch (125), B.C. Forbes (127), Edwin Markham (129), Richard Nixon (130), Mary Kay Ash (134), Louis D. Brandels (137), Arnold Glasow (138), J.C. Penney (140, 143), Ruth Boorstin (141), Conrad Hilton (142), Washington Irving (144), Francis Bacon (145), Robert Townsend (146), Alexander Chase (147), Albert Einstein (148), Edward John Phelps (149), Mary Gardiner Brainard (150), Charles C. Noble (151), Walt Disney (157)

Introduction

God's Little Instruction Book for the Workplace is an inspirational collection of quotes and Scriptures that will motivate those in the workplace to live a meaningful, productive and happy life while inspiring them to strive for excellence and character in living.

Appealing to those in all vocations and career fields, this little book is power packed with dynamic quotes which are coupled with the wisdom of the ages, God's Word.

This little book is designed to be fun to read, yet thought-provoking, supplying those in the workplace with godly insight on numerous topics vital to life. You will find familiar and unfamiliar quotes covering subjects such as career achievement, excellence, character and integrity in living, and finding real success in life. An inspirational verse is included after each quote, so you can read what the instruction manual of life, the Bible, has to say about that topic.

God's Little Instruction Book for the Workplace will help those in the workplace to reach for excellence as they meet the challenges of the future in their job or career.

The secret of success is to do the common things uncommonly well.

Do you see a man skilled in his work? He will serve before kings; he will not serve before obscure men.
Proverbs 22:29 NIV

The way to get to the top is to get off your bottom.

The soul of a lazy man desire, and has nothing;
but the soul of the diligent shall be made rich.
Proverbs 13:4 NKJV

Never, never, never...give up.

—————•—————

And let us not grow weary while doing good,
for in due season we shall reap if we do not lose heart.
Galatians 6:9 NKJV

To love what you do and feel that it matters – how could anything be more fun?

‹———·—›

When you eat the labor of your hands, you shall be happy,
and it shall be well with you.
Psalm 128:2 NKJV

The test of a first-rate work is that you finish it.

I have fought a good fight, I have finished my course....
2 Timothy 4:7

Dreams don't work
unless you do.

—▸———◂—

The desire of the sluggard puts him to death,
for his hands refuse to work.
Proverbs 21:25 NAS

Clear your mind of can't.

I can do all things through Christ who strengthens me.
Philippians 4:13 NKJV

Laziness travels so slowly, that poverty soon overtakes him.

--•--

Yet a little sleep, a little slumber, a little folding of the hands to sleep: so shall thy poverty come as one that travelleth; and thy want as an armed man.
Proverbs 24:33-34

Life is a coin. You can spend it anyway you wish, but you can only spend it once.

—+»—•—«+—

...For what is your life? It is even a vapor that appears for a little time and then vanishes away.
James 4:14 NKJV

Diligence is the mother of good fortune.

...the hand of the diligent makes rich.
Proverbs 10:4 NKJV

Lord, grant that I may always desire more than I can accomplish.

━━◆━━

...forgetting what lies behind and reaching forward to what lies ahead....
Philippians 3:13 NAS

Unhappiness is in not knowing what we want and killing ourselves to get it.

*What profit hath a man of all his labour
which he taketh under the sun?*
Ecclesiastes 1:3

Efficiency is doing things right. Effectiveness is doing the right thing.

Do what is right and good in the sight of the Lord, so that it may go well with you....
Deuteronomy 6:18 NRSV

A statue has never been set up in honor of a critic.

Let us not therefore judge one another....
Romans 14:13

Don't equate activity with efficiency.

Let all things be done decently and in order.
1 Corinthians 14:40

The most wasted of all days
is that on which one
has not laughed.

A happy heart makes the face cheerful, but heartache crushes the spirit.
Proverbs 15:13 NKJV

You can accomplish more in one hour with God than one lifetime without Him.

Walk in wisdom...redeeming the time.
Colossians 4:5

A great man is always willing to be little.

———✦———

But the greatest among you shall be your servant.
Matthew 23:11 NAS

An honest man's word is as good as his bond.

...let your "Yes" be "Yes," and your "No," "No,"....
James 5:12 NKJV

An unused life is an early death.

—•—

The fool folds his hands and consumes his own flesh.
Ecclesiastes 4:5 NAS

In the long run men hit only what they aim at.

Therefore I do not run uncertainly – without definite aim.
1 Corinthians 9:26a AMP

Enthusiasm is contagious. It's difficult to remain neutral or indifferent in the presence of a positive thinker.

—>——•——<—

Finally, brethren, whatever is true...honorable...right...pure... lovely...of good repute, if there is any excellence and if anything worthy of praise, let your mind dwell on these things.
Philippians 4:8 NAS

Find out what you love to do and you will never have to work another day in your life.

...Stand at the crossroads and look; ask for the ancient paths, ask where the good way is, and walk in it, and you will find rest for your souls.
Jeremiah 6:16a NIV

Experience is not what happens to a man, it's what a man does with what happens to him.

For whatever is born of God overcomes the world; and this is the victory that has overcome the world – our faith.
1 John 5:4 NAS

The person who knows "how"
will always have a job.
The person who knows "why"
will always be his boss.

❧

How much better to get wisdom than gold!
And to get understanding is to be chosen rather than silver.
Proverbs 16:16 NKJV

Develop the hunter's attitude, ...wherever you go, there are ideas waiting to be discovered.

━━•━━

For every one who keeps on asking receives, and he who keeps on seeking finds, and to him who keeps on knocking it will be opened.
Matthew 7:8 AMP

Take first things first.
That process often reduces the most complex human problems to manageable proportions.

—————

But seek ye first the kingdom of God, and his righteousness; and all these things shall be added unto you.
Matthew 6:33

Courage is resistance to fear, mastery of fear. Not the absence of fear.

Therefore, take up the full armor of God, that you may
be able to resist in the evil day, and having done everything,
to stand firm. Stand firm therefore....
Ephesians 6:13-14 NAS

The business of finding fault is very easy, and that of doing better very difficult.

Therefore you are without excuse, every man of you who passes judgment, for in that you judge another, you condemn yourself; for you who judge practice the same things.
Romans 2:1 NAS

Remember the difference between a boss and a leader: a boss says "Go!" – a leader says "Let's go!"

...Let us go up at once, and possess it; for we are well able to overcome it.
Numbers 13:30

Some people succeed
because they are destined to,
but most people succeed
because they are determined to.

Seest thou a man diligent in his business? He shall stand before kings....
Proverbs 22:29

He who has a *why* to live can bear almost any *how*.

━━━◦━━━

Never forget your promises to me your servant,
for they are my only hope. They give me strength
in all my troubles; how they refresh and revive me!
Psalm 119:49-50 TLB

Nothing is particularly hard if you divide it into small jobs.

...he [Abram] divided his forces against them by night, he and his servants, and defeated them, and pursued them....
Genesis 14:15 NAS

It is the character of very few men to honor without envy a friend who has prospered.

A friend loves at all times....
Proverbs 17:17 NRSV

A man who does not read good books has no advantage over the man who *can't* read them.

*Apply thine heart unto instruction, and thine ears
to the words of knowledge.*
Proverbs 23:12

Life can't give me joy and peace;
it's up to me to will it. Life just
gives me time and space;
it's up to me to fill it.

·———·———·

...I have set before you life and death, the blessing and the curse;
therefore choose life, that you and your descendants may live.
Deuteronomy 30:19 AMP

Never allow your sense of self
to become associated with
your sense of job. If your job
vanishes, your self doesn't.

—————

*What advantage does man have in all his work which he does
under the sun? A generation goes and a generation comes,
but the earth remains forever.*
Ecclesiastes 1:3-4 NAS

Men for the sake of getting a living forget to live.

...every man should eat and drink, and enjoy the good of all his labour, it is the gift of God.
Ecclesiastes 3:13

The art of being wise is the art of knowing what to overlook.

A man's wisdom gives him patience;
it is to his glory to overlook an offense.
Proverbs 19:11 NIV

We improve ourselves by victories over our self. There must be contests, and we must win.

—•—

Now every athlete who goes into training conducts himself temperately and restricts himself in all things. They do it to win a wreath that will soon wither, but we [do it to receive a crown of eternal blessedness] that cannot wither.
1 Corinthians 9:25 AMP

He that has learned to obey will know how to command.

And the Lord shall make thee the head, and not the tail;
and thou shalt be above only, and thou shalt not be beneath;
if that thou hearken unto the commandments of the Lord thy God,
which I command thee this day, to observe and to do them.
Deuteronomy 28:13

Triumph is just "umph" added to try.

———•———

And let us not be weary in well doing: for in due season
we shall reap, if we faint not.
Galatians 6:9

There is no failure except in no longer trying.

—————•·•—————

Let us hold fast the confession of our hope
without wavering, for He who promised is faithful.
Hebrews 10:23 NKJV

He has achieved success who has lived well, laughed often, and loved much.

Go then, eat your bread in happiness, and drink your wine with a cheerful heart; for God has already approved your works.
Ecclesiastes 9:7 NAS

People don't care how much you know, until they know how much you care...about them.

———•———

And though I have the gift of prophecy, and understand
all mysteries, and all knowledge; and though I have all faith,
so I could remove mountains, and have not charity, I am nothing.
1 Corinthians 13:2

You cannot steal second base while keeping one foot on first base.

—>—•—<—

A double minded man is unstable in all his ways.
James 1:8

The size of your success is determined by the size of your belief.

Everything is possible for him who believes.
Mark 9:23b NIV

Be great in the little things.

——•——

He who is faithful in a very little thing is faithful also in much; and he
who is unrighteous in a very little thing is unrighteous also in much.
Luke 16:10 NAS

Opportunities are seldom labeled.

As we have therefore opportunity, let us do good unto all men, especially unto them who are of the household of faith.
Galatians 6:10

Many a man has found the acquisition of wealth only a change, not an end, of miseries.

He who loves money will not be satisfied with money,
nor he who loves abundance with its income. This too is vanity.
Ecclesiastes 5:10 NAS

I am defeated, and know it,
if I meet any human being
from whom I find myself
unable to learn anything.

A wise man will hear, and will increase learning;
and a man of understanding shall attain unto wise counsels.
Proverbs 1:5

Success seems to be largely a matter of hanging on after others have let go.

Let us hold fast the confession of our hope without wavering, for He who promised is faithful.
Hebrews 10:23 NKJV

If you keep saying that things are going to be bad, you have a chance of being a prophet.

Thou art snared with the words of thy mouth,
thou art taken with the words of thy mouth.
Proverbs 6:2

A great deal of good can be done in the world if one is not too careful who gets the credit.

–→—•—←–

So then, whether you eat or drink, or whatever you may do,
do all for the honor and glory of God.
1 Corinthians 10:31 AMP

Show me a man who cannot bother to do little things and I'll show you a man who cannot be trusted to do big things.

—————

...You have been faithful and trustworthy over a little;
I will put you in charge of much.
Matthew 25:21b AMP

Faith is daring the soul to go beyond what the eyes can see.

———•———

Now faith is the substance of things hoped for,
the evidence of things not seen.
Hebrews 11:1 NKJV

Good words are worth much, and cost little.

Pleasant words are a honeycomb,
sweet to the soul and healing to the bones.
Proverbs 16:24 NAS

I don't know the secret to success but the key to failure is to try to please everyone.

No one can serve two masters; for either he will hate the one and love the other, or he will hold to one and despise the other.
Matthew 6:24a NAS

It is a mistake to look
too far ahead. Only one link
of the chain of destiny can
be handled at a time.

———◆———

Therefore do not be anxious for tomorrow;
for tomorrow will care for itself.
Each day has enough trouble of its own.
Matthew 6:34 NAS

It's the job that's never started that takes longest to finish.

———•———

The way of the sluggard is blocked with thorns,
but the path of the upright is a highway.
Proverbs 15:19 NIV

Business is like a wheelbarrow. Nothing ever happens until you start pushing.

He who has a slack hand becomes poor,
but the hand of the diligent makes rich.
Proverbs 10:4 NKJV

The world is full of willing people: some willing to work, the rest willing to let them.

*Then he said to his disciples, "The harvest is plentiful,
but the workers are few."*
Matthew 9:37 NAS

The most difficult secret for a man to keep is the opinion he has of himself.

———•———

...I warn every one among you...not to have
an exaggerated opinion of his own importance;
but to rate his ability with sober judgment....
Romans 12:3 AMP

No one ever said on their deathbed: I wish I would have spent more time at work!

―――•――――

Then I considered all that my hands had done and the toil I had spent in doing it, and again, all was vanity and a chasing after wind....
Ecclesiastes 2:11 NRSV

No one is useless in this world who lightens the burden of it to anyone else.

———

Bear ye one another's burdens, and so fulfil the law of Christ.
Galatians 6:2

Do not follow where the path
may lead – go instead where
there is no path and leave a trail.

＊＞━＊・＊━＜＋

Your ears shall hear a word behind you, saying,
"This is the way, walk in it...."
Isaiah 30:21 NKJV

There is one thing alone
that stands the brunt of life
throughout its length:
a quiet conscience.

...if our hearts do not condemn us, we have confidence before God.
1 John 3:21 NIV

My obligation is to do the right thing. The rest is in God's hands.

If you know that he is righteous, you may be sure that everyone who does right has been born of him.
1 John 2:29 RSV

When you soar like an eagle, you attract hunters.

Be of sober spirit, be on the alert. Your adversary, the devil, prowls about like a roaring lion, seeking someone to devour.
1 Peter 5:8 NAS

Those that have done nothing in life are not qualified to be judge of those that have done little.

Do not judge, or you too will be judged. For in the same way you judge others, you will be judged....
Matthew 7:1-2 NIV

Every Christian needs half
an hour of prayer each day
except when he is busy.
Then he needs an hour.

*Evening and morning and at noon I will pray, and cry aloud, and He
shall hear my voice.*
Psalm 55:17 NKJV

Expect great things *from* God.
Attempt great things *for* God.

———

Truly, truly, I say to you, he who believes in Me, the works that I do shall he do also; and greater works than these shall he do; because I go to the Father.
John 14:12 NAS

Ah, but a man's reach *should* exceed his grasp.

✦

...but this one thing I do: forgetting what lies behind and straining forward to what lies ahead, I press on toward the goal....
Philippians 3:13-14 NRSV

Anybody can do their best. God helps us to do better than our best.

Now glory be to God who by his mighty power at work within us is able to do far more than we would ever dare to ask or even dream of....
Ephesians 3:20 TLB

Shallow men believe in luck...strong men believe in cause and effect.

—

Be not deceived; God is not mocked:
for whatsoever a man soweth, that shall he also reap.
Galatians 6:7

Dost thou love life? Then do not squander time, for that is the stuff life is made of.

Remember how short my time is....
Psalm 89:47

Don't let your learning lead to knowledge, let your learning lead to action.

...be ye doers of the word, and not hearers only,
deceiving your own selves.
James 1:22

Procrastination is the thief of time.

———•———

He also that is slothful in his work is brother to him that is a great waster.
Proverbs 18:9

Forget your opponents; always play against par.

—•—

For we wrestle not against flesh and blood....
Ephesians 6:12

Never play not to lose; always play to win.

—————

But thanks be to God, Who gives us the victory –
making us conquerors – through our Lord Jesus Christ.
1 Corinthians 15:57 AMP

Saddle your dreams before you ride 'em.

—✦—

...Write the vision, and make it plain upon tables,
that he may run that readeth it.
Habakkuk 2:2

You do not lead by hitting people over the head – that's assault, not leadership.

And the servant of the Lord must not strive; but be gentle unto all men, apt to teach, patient.
2 Timothy 2:24

An inconvenience is only an adventure wrongly considered.

*For the gate is small, and the way is narrow
that leads to life, and few are those who find it.*
Matthew 7:14 NAS

Destiny is not a matter of chance,
it is a matter of choice.
It is not a thing to be waited for;
it is a thing to be achieved.

*I press toward the goal for the prize of
the upward call of God in Christ Jesus.*
Philippians 3:14 NKJV

Imagination was given to man to compensate him for what he is not. A sense of humor was provided to console him for what he is.

>—·—<

A merry heart doeth good like a medicine....
Proverbs 17:22

Far and away the best prize that life offers is the chance to work hard at work worth doing.

Wealth obtained by fraud dwindles,
but the one who gathers by labor increases it.
Proverbs 13:11 NAS

Do not persist in folly. It is not a badge of character to continue down the wrong road.

The way of a fool is right in his own eyes,
but he who heeds counsel is wise.
Proverbs 12:15 NKJV

Man cannot discover new oceans unless he has the courage to lose sight of the shore.

—•—

Now the just shall live by faith: but if any man draw back,
my soul shall have no pleasure in him.
Hebrews 10:38

Unless you try to do something beyond what you have already mastered, you will never grow.

*...but one thing I do: forgetting what lies behind
and reaching forward to what lies ahead.*
Philippians 3:13 NAS

I think the one lesson I have learned is that there is no substitute for paying attention.

—⊱·⊰—

A wise man will hear and increase in learning,
and a man of understanding will acquire wise counsel.
Proverbs 1:5 NAS

When we do the best that we can, we never know what miracle is wrought in our life, or the life of another.

›——·——‹

And whatever you do, do it heartily, as to the Lord and not to men.
Colossians 3:23 NKJV

In life as in a football game, the principle to follow is: hit the line hard.

———»·»—«·«———

Whatever your hand finds to do, do it with all your might.
Ecclesiastes 9:10 NIV

Nothing will ever be attempted if all possible objections must first be overcome.

———•———

The sluggard says, "There is a lion in the road!
A lion is in the open square!"
Proverbs 26:13 NAS

He who conquers others is strong. He who conquers himself is mighty.

He who is slow to anger is better than the mighty,
and he who rules his spirit than he who takes a city.
Proverbs 16:32 NKJV

Don't let "Well done" on your tombstone mean you were cremated!

―――・――

His lord said unto him, "Well done, thou good an faithful servant: thou hast been faithful over a few things, I will make thee ruler over many things....
Matthew 25:21

What counts is not the number of hours you put in, but how much you put in the hours.

Therefore be careful how you walk, not as unwise men, but as wise, making the most of your time, because the days are evil.
Ephesians 5:15-16 NAS

The way for a young man to rise is to improve himself every way he can....

A wise man will hear, and will increase learning;
and a man of understanding shall attain unto wise counsels.
Proverbs 1:5

The only preparation for tomorrow is the right use of today.

Take therefore no thought for the morrow:
for the morrow shall take thought for the things of itself.
Matthew 6:34a

A man of honor regrets a discreditable act even when it has worked.

⟶ • ⟵

A wise man's heart directs him toward the right,
but the foolish man's heart directs him toward the left.
Ecclesiastes 10:2 NAS

None will improve your lot, if you yourselves do not.

Study to shew thyself approved unto God....
2 Timothy 2:15

Whether you think you can or you can't, you are right.

For as he thinketh in his heart, so is he....
Proverbs 23:7

The recipe for perpetual
ignorance is: be satisfied
with your opinions and
content with your knowledge.

—

Do you see a man wise in his own eyes?
There is more hope for a fool than for him.
Proverbs 26:12 NAS

Begin to act boldly. The moment one definitely commits oneself, heaven moves in his behalf.

Let us therefore come boldly unto the throne of grace, that we may obtain mercy, and find grace to help in time of need.
Hebrews 4:16

Waste no more time arguing what a good man should be. Be one.

...be an example (pattern) for the believers,
in speech, in conduct, in love, in faith, and in purity.
1 Timothy 4:12 AMP

Take calculated risks. That is quite different from being rash.

The plans of the diligent lead surely to advantage,
but everyone who is hasty comes surely to poverty.
Proverbs 21:5 NAS

There is no substitute for hard work.

Do you see a man skilled in his work? He will serve before kings;
he will not serve before obscure men.
Proverbs 22:29 NIV

Talk low, talk slow,
and don't say too much.

—————

Do not be hasty in word or impulsive in thought
to bring up a matter in the presence of God.
Ecclesiastes 5:2a NAS

Indecision is often worse than the wrong action.

———

A double minded man is unstable in all his ways.
James 1:8

It is better to take a risk now than to always live in fear.

—◆——◆——◆—

*...The Lord is my helper, and I will not fear
what man shall do unto me.*
Hebrews 13:6

Carpe diem – seize the day!

—◦—

...the kingdom of heaven suffereth violence,
and the violent take it by force.
Matthew 11:12

Genius is divine perseverance.

...having done all, to stand. Stand therefore....
Ephesians 6:13-14

No plan is worth the paper it is printed on unless it starts you doing something.

*Write the vision and make it plain on tablets,
that he may run who reads it.*
Habakkuk 2:2 NKJV

"I can't do it" never yet accomplished anything; "I will try" has performed wonders.

———·———

I can do everything through him who gives me strength.
Philippians 4:13 NIV

Protect your own credibility.
One of the highest accolades
is the comment, "If he says so,
you can bank on it."

—•—

Righteous lips are the delight of kings;
and they love him that speaketh right.
Proverbs 16:13

No matter what you do, do your best at it. If you're going to be a bum, be the best bum there is.

And whatsoever ye do, do it heartily, as to the Lord, and not unto men.
Colossians 3:23

The grass may look greener on the other side, but it still has to be mowed.

...and be content with such things as ye have....
Hebrews 13:5

Identify your highest skill
and devote your time
to performing it.

*Wherefore the rather, brethren, give diligence to make your calling
and election sure: for if ye do these things, ye shall never fall.*
2 Peter 1:10

Even a woodpecker owes his success to the fact that he uses his head.

The wise have eyes in their head, but fools walk in darkness.
Ecclesiastes 2:14a NRSV

Millions saw the apple fall, but Newton was the one who asked *why*.

...get wisdom: and with all thy getting get understanding.
Proverbs 4:7

Every job is a self-portrait of the person who does it. Autograph your work with excellence.

———

Many...have done well, but you excel them all.
Proverbs 31:29 NKJV

There is more credit and satisfaction in being a first-rate truck driver than a tenth-rate executive.

The sluggard craves and gets nothing,
but the desires of the diligent are fully satisfied.
Proverbs 13:4 NIV

The man who is born with a talent which he was meant to use finds his greatest happiness in using it.

*But life is worth nothing unless I use it for doing
the work assigned me by the Lord Jesus....*
Acts 20:24 TLB

For all your days prepare,
and meet them ever alike;
when you are the anvil, bear –
when you are the hammer, strike.

*Study to shew thyself approved unto God,
a workman that needeth not to be ashamed....*
2 Timothy 2:15

A man is not finished when he is defeated. He is finished when he quits.

And let us not be weary in well doing: for in due season we shall reap, if we faint not.
Galatians 6:9

The greatest achievements are those that benefit others.

―――•―――

To be the greatest, be a servant.
Matthew 23:11b TLB

Genius is one percent inspiration and ninety-nine percent perspiration.

For just as the body without the spirit is dead,
so also faith without works is dead.
James 2:26 NAS

We make a living by what we get – we make a life by what we give.

...It is more blessed to give than to receive.
Acts 20:35 NAS

Honesty is the cornerstone of all success, without which confidence and ability to perform shall cease to exist.

+>—•—<+

Let me be weighed on honest scales, that God may know my integrity.
Job 31:6 NKJV

If a task is once begun,
never leave it till it's done.
Be the labor great or small,
do it well or not at all.

Whatever your hand finds to do, do it with your might....
Ecclesiastes 9:10 NKJV

Our days are identical suitcases –
all the same size – but some
people can pack more into
them than others.

―▸ • ◂―

...making the most of your time....
Ephesians 5:16 NAS

Most of the things worth
doing in the world had
been declared impossible
before they were done.

...With men this is impossible; but with God all things are possible.
Matthew 19:26

In life, as in football, you won't go far unless you know where the goal posts are.

Where there is no vision, the people perish....
Proverbs 29:18

In the race to be better or best, don't forget to enjoy the journey!

Be happy...and rejoice and be glad-hearted continually....
1 Thessalonians 5:16 AMP

It's one of the hardest things in the world to accept criticism...and turn it to your advantage.

Now no chastening seems to be joyful for the present, but painful; nevertheless, afterward it yields the peaceable fruit of righteousness to those who have been trained by it.
Hebrews 12:11 NKJV

Here is a piece of advice
that is worth a king's crown:
To hold your head up, hold
your overhead down.

———•———

Any enterprise is built by wise planning, becomes strong through common sense, and profits wonderfully by keeping abreast of the facts.
Proverbs 24:3-4 TLB

Success seems to be connected
with action. Successful people
keep moving. They make
mistakes, but they don't quit.

<hr />

...let us throw off everything that hinders...and let us run with persever-
ance the race marked out for us.
Hebrews 12:1 NIV

Give me a stock clerk *with*
a goal, and I will give you
a man who will make history.
Give me a man *without* a goal
and I will give you a stock clerk.

━━━•━━━

*...fixing our eyes on Jesus...who for the joy set before Him endured the
cross...and has sat down at the right hand of the throne of God.*
Hebrews 12:2 NAS

Great minds have purpose; others have wishes.

"For I know the plans I have for you," declares the Lord,
"plans to prosper you...to give you a hope and a future."
Jeremiah 29:11 NIV

A wise man will make more opportunity than he finds.

A man's gift maketh room for him, and bringeth him before great men.
Proverbs 18:16

Make every decision as if you owned the whole company.

He that handleth a matter wisely shall find good....
Proverbs 16:20

He who considers his work beneath him will be above doing it well.

—•—

The greatest among you will be your servant.
Matthew 23:11 NRSV

Success is the result of working hard, playing hard, and keeping your mouth shut.

...even a fool is thought to be wise when he is silent.
It pays him to keep his mouth shut.
Proverbs 17:28 TLB

The man who makes no mistakes does not normally make anything.

*Though he fall, he shall not utterly be cast down:
for the Lord upholdeth him with his hand.*
Psalm 37:24

I would rather walk with God in the dark than go alone in the light.

—⊷⊶•⊷⊶—

Even when walking through the dark valley of death I will not be afraid, for you are close beside me, guarding, guiding all the way.
Psalm 23:4 TLB

You must have long-range goals to keep you from being frustrated by short-range failures.

For the vision is yet for an appointed time....
Though it tarries, wait for it; because it will surely come....
Habakkuk 2:3 NKJV

It takes more to plow a field
than merely turning it over
in your mind.

—·—

...faith by itself, if it is not accompanied by action, is dead.
James 2:17 NIV

True contentment is the power of getting out of any situation all that there is in it.

I have learned the secret of being content in any and every situation....
Philippians 4:12b NIV

People may doubt what you say, but they will believe what you do.

―――――・――――

My little children, let us not love in word,
neither in tongue; but in deed and in truth.
1 John 3:18

The right angle to approach a difficult problem is the "try-angle."

I can do all things through Christ who strengthens me.
Philippians 4:13 NKJV

The difference between ordinary and *extra*ordinary is that little extra.

*In a race, everyone runs but only one person
gets first prize. So run your race to win.*
1 Corinthians 9:24 TLB

All our dreams can come true – if we have the courage to pursue them.

—————

...Be strong and courageous, and act; do not fear nor be dismayed, for the Lord God, my God, is with you.
1 Chronicles 23:20a NAS

References

Unless otherwise indicated, all Scripture quotations are taken from the *King James Version* of the Bible.

Scripture quotations marked NIV are taken from the *Holy Bible, New International Version* ®. NIV ®. Copyright © 1973, 1978, 1984 by International Bible Society. Used by permission of Zondervan Publishing House. All rights reserved.

Scripture quotations marked AMP are taken from *The Amplified Bible. Old Testament* copyright © 1965 by Zondervan Publishing House, Grand Rapids, MI. *New Testament* copyright © 1958 by *The Lockman Foundation*, La Habra, California. Used by permission.

Verses marked TLB are taken from *The Living Bible*, copyright © 1971. Used by permission of Tyndale House Publishers, Inc., Wheaton, Illinois 60189. All rights reserved.

Scripture quotations marked NAS are taken from the *New American Standard Bible*. Copyright © The Lockman Foundation 1960, 1962, 1963, 1968, 1971, 1972, 1973, 1975, 1977. Used by permission.

Scripture quotations marked NRSV are taken from *The New Revised Standard Version Bible*, copyright © 1989 by the Division of Christian Education of the Churches of Christ in the United States of America and is used by permission.

Scripture quotations marked NKJV are taken from *The New King James Version* of the Bible. Copyright © 1979, 1980, 1982, 1994 by Thomas Nelson, Inc., Publishers. Used by permission.

Dear Reader:

If you would like to share with us a couple of your favorite quotes or ideas on the subject of *being successful in the workplace* we'd love to hear from you. Our address is:

Honor Books
P.O. Box 55388, Dept. J.
Tulsa, Oklahoma 74155

Additional copies of this book and other titles
in the *God's Little Instruction Book* series
are available at your local bookstore.

God's Little Instruction Book
God's Little Instruction Book II
God's Little Instruction Book for Mom
God's Little Instruction Book for Dad
God's Little Instruction Book for Graduates
God's Little Instruction Book for Students
God's Little Instruction Book for Kids
God's Little Instruction Book for Couples
God's Little Instruction Book — Special Gift Edition
God's Little Instruction Book Daily Calendar

Honor Books
P.O. Box 55388
Tulsa, Oklahoma 74155